Leonardo's
ABC

Sharing Leonardo da Vinci
with Children

Written by Carolyn Cinami DeCristofano

Sharing Leonardo da Vinci with Children

Any child's persistent questions reveal his or her similarity to Leonardo da Vinci (1452-1519). Leonardo voraciously explored science, invention, and art. At the heart of his activities was a childlike reliance on observation, curiosity, and learning through experience.

Leonardo's notebooks—loose leaf sheets filled with questions, notes, sketches, drawings, and diagrams—show us how he looked at and thought about the world. Like Leonardo, children have the capacity to combine many different disciplines in their everyday "work" and play. They build and invent, they respond to nature through art, and they have a seemingly endless inclination to wonder about everything, from the shape of a leaf to the distance of the stars.

All too often, historical figures like Leonardo seem remote and inaccessible to children. We hope this book will "span a great length" between Leonardo and children by connecting his images and ideas to the familiar objects and experiences of a child's world. A quintessential life-long learner, Leonardo can inspire children and adults alike to cherish and forever hold on to the qualities that they share with him.

Leonardo did very many things, so curious was he!
Turn the page to learn about him in this ABC.

Leonardo drew ARCHES

and studied their strength,

A *A*

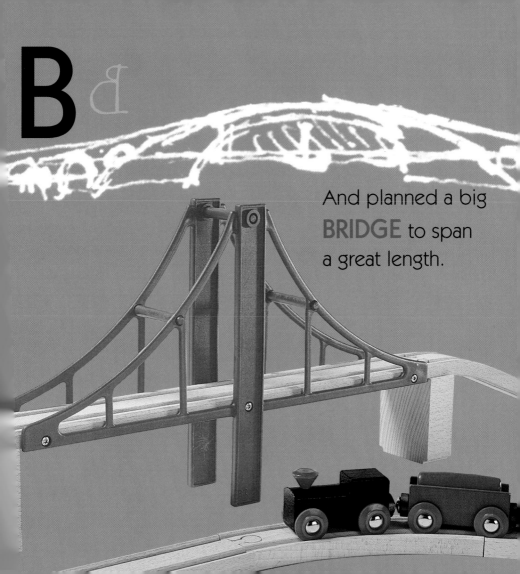

B b

And planned a big **BRIDGE** to span a great length.

C

He watched and
sketched **CATS**,
with every detail
complete,

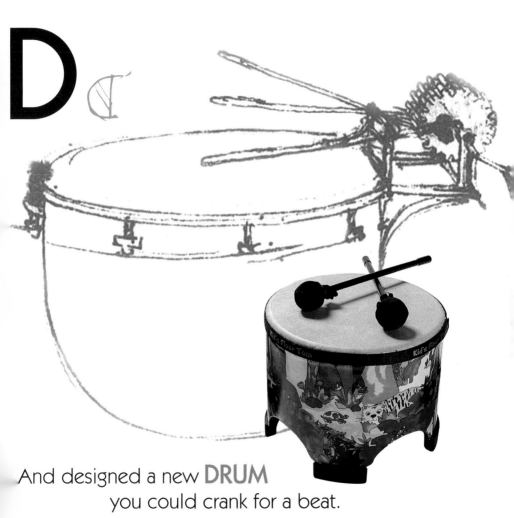

D

And designed a new **DRUM**
you could crank for a beat.

E

Leonardo saw nature
        with a very keen EYE,

F f

And imagined a FLYING MACHINE

soaring in the sky.

G

He tinkered with GEARS and mechanical force,

H h

...nd planned a huge
statue of a rider
and **HORSE**

I

Leonardo invented **INSTRUMENTS**
with hammers and strings,

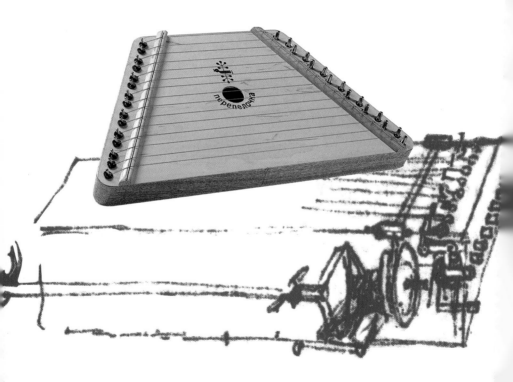

J

And drew the bony JOINTS
of arms, legs, and wings.

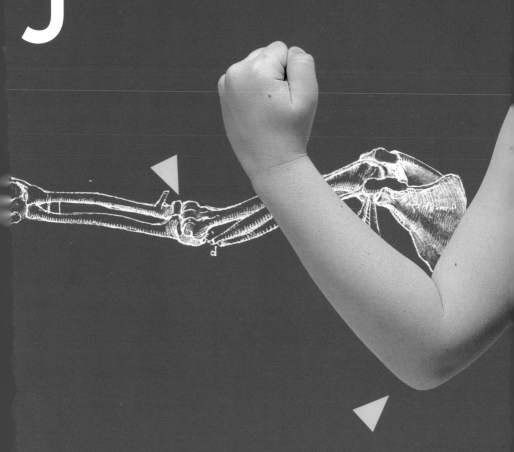

He drew intricate KNOTS, every loop, turn, and twist,

K

And wrote his LETTERS ƧЯƎTTƎ⅃
backwards in his manuscripts.

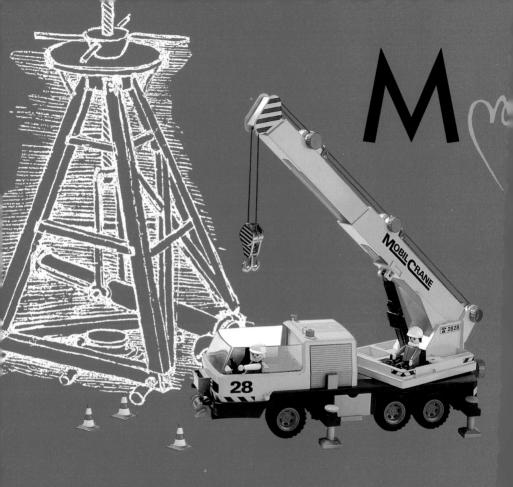

M

Leonardo dreamed of MACHINES—
such great gadgets he designed,

And noted many

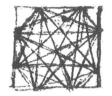

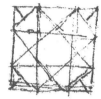

PA
TT
ER
NS

that to others
were concealed.

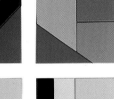

Q

What do I see?

What do I see?

Leonardo asked QUESTIONS
like "Why?" and "How can it be?"

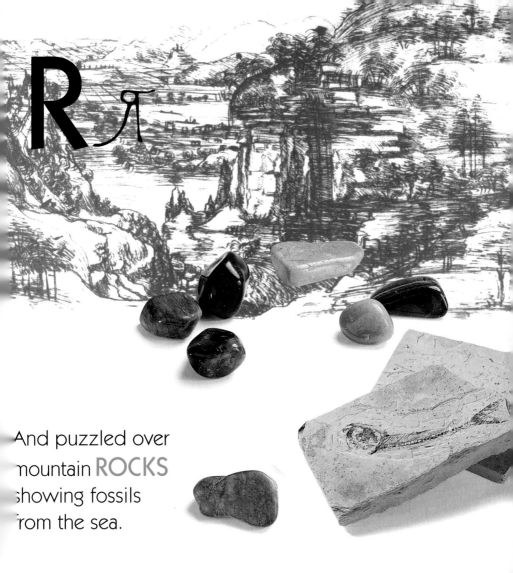

R ᴙ

And puzzled over
mountain ROCKS
showing fossils
from the sea.

S s

He thought of weights and balance like a **SEE-SAW** with two men,

T t

And looked at branching
TREES—how they
curve, how they bend.

Leonardo gazed at the
UNIVERSE—the moon, stars, and sun;

U

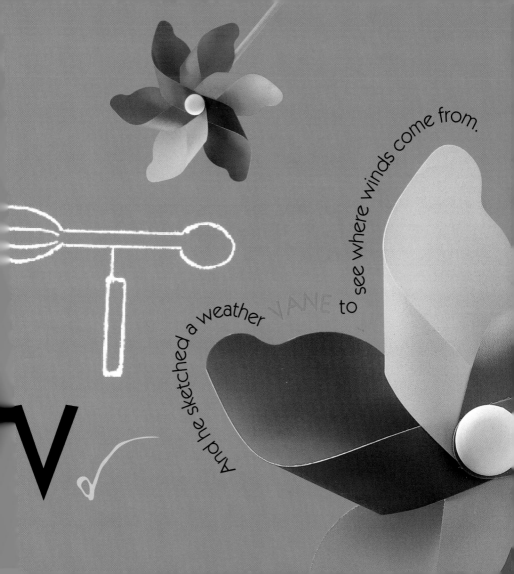

And he sketched a weather VANE to see where winds come from.

He watched WAVES in water and noted their effects,

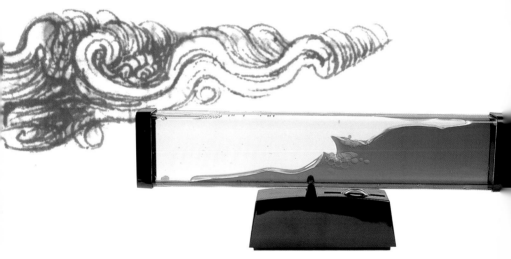

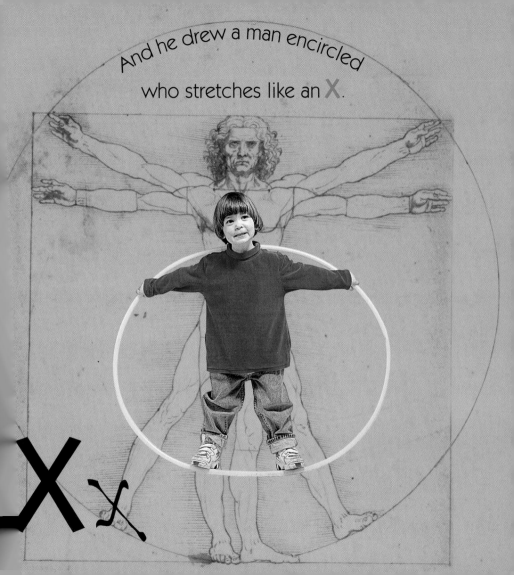

And he drew a man encircled

who stretches like an X.

Xx

Yy

Leonardo might have
drawn himself —
you can too!

Z

And he drew so many animals,
they'd nearly fill a ZOO!

Leonardo did very many things, so curious was he!
What ideas do you dream about from A all the way to Z?

On most pages of this book, letters written in Leonardo's hand appear next to their print counterparts. These script letters were taken from Leonardo's notebooks. Handwritten versions of J, U, and W were unavailable.

Concept and design by Kaminsky Design, Boston, MA
Written by Carolyn Cinami DeCristofano

Leonardo da Vinci images provided by:
Archive Photos, New York
Corbis Corporation, Bellevue, WA
Dover Publications, New York
EMB Service for Publishers, Lucerne, Switzerland
Superstock, New York

Printed in Mexico
10 9 8 7 6 5 4 3 2 1

Aa Bb Cc

Gg Hh Ii J

Nn Oo Pp

Uu Vv Wv